BEIRUT
THE CITY AT A GLANCE

CW00552019

BIEL
Beirut's provisional exhibition
centre stands on reclaimed lan
built from the rubble of the po
Beirut New Waterfront

Maghen Abraham Synagogue
Funded by a Calcuttan Jew in 19
sole synagogue reopened its do
Wadi Abu Jamil Street

Grain Silo
Designed by Rodolphe Elias, this towering
1960 silo holds up to 120,000 tons of grain.
Beirut Port

Grand Serail
This former Ottoman army barracks now
serves as the office of the prime minister.
Al-Jaish Street

Mohammad al-Amin Mosque
Although it looks old architecturally,
the city's largest mosque dates to 2008.
Bechara el-Khoury Street

Azariye Building
André Leconte's sprawling sandstone office
and commercial complex, finished in 1953,
is under the ownership of Beirut's Lazarists.
Amir Bachir Street

Saint Gregory Cathedral
Home to the seat of the Armenian Catholic
Patriarchate of Cilicia, this Central Beirut
church was completed in 1909.
Charles Debbas Street

Sassine Square
A busy intersection at the heart of the
Ashrafiye neighbourhood, Sassine Square
is hugely popular for its coffee shops.

INTRODUCTION
THE CHANGING FACE OF THE URBAN SCENE

Fascinating and dramatic, Beirut is rarely what people expect but always much more than they imagined. Understanding it, however, is another story. It's Middle Eastern and Mediterranean. A 6,000-year-old city, primarily built in the 1950s; home to the most active cultural scene in the region but only two public museums. It has a violent past and a vibrant nightlife, so gets portrayed either as the city of night or the city of nightmare. There are, as every excitable foreign journalist is eager to remind us, mullahs and movie-houses, hijabs and high heels.

If that is a revelation, it is not to Beirut. A city of everyone, belonging to no one, which plays the interstices for all that they are worth, it is not about binaries. Or unities. With 1.9 million magnificent individuals who only agree to disagree, and 18 different religious communities, each with a distinct idea of how to live, Beirut invented the art of navigating contradictions.

This is where the Middle East tries on new things, from the most recent fashions to the latest political ideas. It's where everything is possible, even if it isn't permitted, and when things are going smoothly, where you can be whoever you want, even if your neighbours don't approve. You could spend a (beautiful) lifetime trying to figure it out, debating the niceties for hours in cafés. Or you could do what the world's first post-nation nation does: learn to accept life as it is and get on with living it. Very well.

ESSENTIAL INFO
FACTS, FIGURES AND USEFUL ADDRESSES

TOURIST OFFICE
Ministry of Tourism
550 Central Bank Street
T 01 340 940
www.lebanon-tourism.gov.lb

TRANSPORT
Car hire
Avis
Army Street
T 01 366 662
www.avis.com.lb
Taxi
Allô Taxi
T 1213
www.allotaxi.com.lb
Servees (shared taxis) can be hailed on the
street. Each person pays for a set distance.

EMERGENCY SERVICES
Ambulance
T 140
Police
T 112
24-hour pharmacy
Mazen Pharmacy
Corniche el-Mazraa/Saeb Salam
T 01 313 362
www.mazenpharmacy.com

EMBASSIES
British Embassy
Armies Street
Zouqaq el-Blatt
Serail Hill
T 01 960 800
www.ukinlebanon.fco.gov.uk
US Embassy
Off Dbayeh Highway
Facing Awkar Municipal Building
T 04 542 600
lebanon.usembassy.gov

POSTAL SERVICES
Post office
Riad el-Solh Street
Shipping
UPS
T 01 218 575
www.ups.com

BOOKS
Beirut by Samir Kassir
(University of California Press)
Beware of Small States
by David Hirst (Faber and Faber)
**Karol Schayer: A Polish Architect
in Beirut** by George Arbid (Birkhäuser)

WEBSITES
Architecture
www.archileb.com
Newspaper
www.dailystar.com.lb

EVENTS
Beirut Art Fair
www.menasart-fair.com
Home Works
www.ashkalalwan.org
International Documentary Festival
www.docudays.com

COST OF LIVING
**Taxi from Beirut-Rafic Hariri
International Airport to Central Beirut**
LBP45,000
Cappuccino
LBP6,000
Packet of cigarettes
LBP2,400
Daily newspaper
LBP5,000
Bottle of champagne
LBP98,000

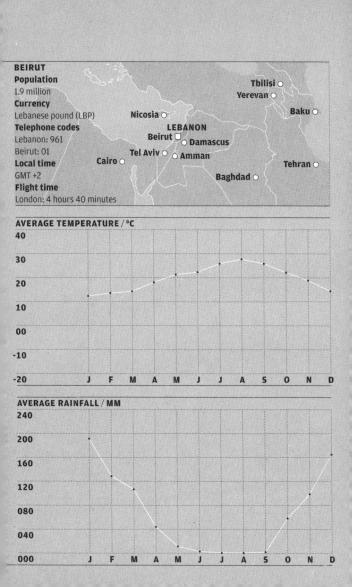

BEIRUT

Population
1.9 million

Currency
Lebanese pound (LBP)

Telephone codes
Lebanon: 961
Beirut: 01

Local time
GMT +2

Flight time
London: 4 hours 40 minutes

Tbilisi
Yerevan
Baku
Nicosia
LEBANON
Beirut
Damascus
Tel Aviv
Cairo
Amman
Tehran
Baghdad

AVERAGE TEMPERATURE / °C

| | J | F | M | A | M | J | J | A | S | O | N | D |

40
30
20
10
00
-10
-20

AVERAGE RAINFALL / MM

| | J | F | M | A | M | J | J | A | S | O | N | D |

240
200
160
120
080
040
000

NEIGHBOURHOODS

THE AREAS YOU NEED TO KNOW AND WHY

To help you navigate the city, we've chosen the most interesting districts (see below and the map inside the back cover) and colour-coded our featured venues, according to their location; those venues that are outside these areas are not coloured.

HAMRA/RAS BEIRUT

Once a modernist byword for sedition and chic, Hamra Street was the Middle East's boulevard of dreams. Today, the district accommodates Beirut's most diverse mix of people. Urban, but no longer cutting-edge, it's filled with fading midcentury architecture, especially near Pigeon Rocks.

GEMMAYZE/MAR MIKHAYEL

A close approximation of what downtown looked like before the wars, these areas are undergoing huge change. Gouraud Street's Ottoman, Mandate and art deco buildings are packed with eateries and cool bars like Torino (see p047). Mar Mikhayel's low(er) rents attract creatives.

MOUSSEITBEH/MAZRAA

Southern Beirut's relatively cramped and crowded apartment blocks are bound to the east by the Hippodrome (see p088) and the (reforested) pinewood Horsh Beirut park. To the west are the luxury towers of Ramlet el-Baida and the only remaining sand beach within city limits.

QANTARI

One of Beirut's oldest areas emptied in the wars, but is now highly sought-after again. Qantari includes the Armenian Haigazian University (Mexico Street, T 349 230), five-star hotels, such as the Phoenicia (see p020), and the city's only synagogue. Herzog & de Meuron and Foster + Partners are among those reshaping its skyline.

CENTRAL BEIRUT

Love it or hate it, downtown is re-emerging as the capital's heart. Amid archaeological remains, handsome religious buildings and Franco-Ottoman architecture, the post-wars reconstruction is accused of creating an elitist enclave. For now, this may be true, but it's a perfect place to wander in wonder.

ZOUQAQ EL-BLATT/BASTA

Historically popular with the elite, who kept grand summer homes here (some of which still exist), and the intelligentsia, this was where the Arab cultural awakening, the Nahda, took shape in the 19th century. Now inhabited by rural migrants, it's better known for the antiques market in Basta.

AIN EL-MREISSE

Mostly taken up by the leafy campus of the AUB (Ras Beirut, T 340 460), the Middle East's first modern university, this strip of the city draws wealthy and expat Lebanese and Arabs. Many own homes in the new towers rising along the Corniche (see p089), where Beirutis come to stroll.

ASHRAFIYE

Until the early noughties, Ashrafiye was of little interest. Then came Monot Street, Beirut's first real nightlife district. ABC mall (Albert Naccash Street, T 212 888) and a host of shops and restaurants, such as Goutons Voir (see p033), secured its ascent. A rash of new high-rises has led to the loss of numerous heritage buildings.

LANDMARKS

THE SHAPE OF THE CITY SKYLINE

Although it's as old as Adam, Beirut has few landmarks. Whether you attribute this to a tumultuous history, which includes seven rounds of natural and human destruction, or deference to natural monuments (the splendid wall of mountains, snow-capped in winter) encircling it, depends on how romantic you are.

For many non-Lebanese, Beirut's most famous places tend towards the infamous. The Holiday Inn and Murr Tower, both strategic vantage points, still stand, though the former should be demolished, to the delight of Beirutis tired of looking up at the mortar holes. Other landmarks are less accessible. The Grand Serail (Al-Jaish Street), the prime minister's office housed in the former Ottoman barracks above the city centre, can't be visited up close. Likewise Résidence des Pins (Abdallah el-Yafi Avenue/ Bechara el-Khoury Street), a fine example of Levantine architecture and where Lebanon's independence was formally declared.

Some buildings can't be missed. The neo-Ottoman Mohammad al-Amin Mosque (Bechara el-Khoury Street), finished in 2007, is so large it's probably visible from space. Something of a political statement, its billowing domes and four minarets made the neighbouring 1894 Maronite Cathedral of Saint Georges (Amir Bachir Street) toy-like in comparison, prompting retaliation with the region's tallest belfry, which was added in the late noughties. *For full addresses, see Resources.*

Abed Clocktower

Designed by Armenian dentist turned architect Mardiros Altounian, who graduated from the École des Beaux Arts in Paris in 1918, this art deco clocktower stands at the centre of Nejmeh Square, Beirut's partial Place de l'Étoile. It sits on top of the old Roman forum, discovered during construction work in the late 1960s. Commissioned by wealthy Lebanese-Mexican émigré Michel el-Abed and gifted to the city in 1933, the sandstone tower has four clock faces, which, with enviable Levantine insouciance, display slightly different versions of the time. Born in Turkey, from where he was forced to flee, Altounian is almost forgotten today, yet he also designed the Lebanese Parliament Building next to the clocktower, the ornate neo-Moorish Daouk Building in Ashrafiye, and a number of villas for Lebanese politicians and Jordanian royalty.
Nejmeh Square

Statue of the Martyrs

What looks like a motorway interchange was once the beating heart of Beirut. Razed post-wars, opening up cinematic views to the mountains, Martyrs' Square is being replanned by Renzo Piano. In the middle is Renato Marino Mazzacurati's tribute to those who perished during the struggle for independence from the Ottomans. Erected in 1958, the statue remained in place during the wars, but was removed in 1996. Riddled with bullet holes, it was taken away for restoration but not put back until 2004, prompting rumours 'political' decisions had prevented its return. It arrived just in time to preside over the protests that finally 'persuaded' Syria to pull out of the country in 2005. Nearby is Mazzacurati's sculpture of Riad al-Solh, co-founder of modern Lebanon. *Martyrs' Square*

Hope of Peace Monument

Lebanon's official war monument offers two modern pleasures in one. The first is André Wogenscky and Maurice Hindieh's 1965 Ministry of Defence. A Brasília-esque beauty (off limits to civilians), its rationalist geometries can be seen on the approach. The second is the late Franco-American artist Arman's Hope of Peace tower, a 32m-tall, 6,000-tonne sandwich of anti-aircraft guns, tanks and armoured cars, partially encased in concrete. Commemorating the 50th anniversary of the founding of the Lebanese army, it was unveiled in 1995 to some controversy. To understand why requires a grasp of geography, recent history and a willingness to read between the lines. The turrets, at various degrees of elevation, all point east over the mountains at Lebanon's largest neighbour.

Damascus Road, Yarze, Baabda

St Georges Hotel

Favoured by John Paul Getty, who ate at The Grill when in town, and royalty of state and silver screen (the kings of Egypt, Iran, Greece; Peter O'Toole, Omar Sharif, Liz and Richard), the St Georges was the most glamorous hotel in the Middle East and, according to some, the world. Completed in 1932 and designed by one of the region's first modernists, Antoine Tabet, who trained in Paris under Monsieur Reinforced Concrete, Auguste Perret, it was surrounded on three sides by the sea, and its terrace boasted one of the finest views around. Today, it is brutally cut off from the Med by Beirut's 6m-high seawall. Sacked in the opening salvoes of the wars, and never reopened, it's a poignant reminder of all Beirut once thought it was.
Wafik Sinno Avenue

HOTELS

WHERE TO STAY AND WHICH ROOMS TO BOOK

Beirut has plenty of hotels, but most are not worth the price you have to pay. The major chains are moving in, which can be both a blessing and a curse, although Lebanon's fluctuating stability often brings new projects to a halt, even as tourist numbers rise inexorably. Consequently, at peak times – Christmas, New Year, Easter, Eid al-Fitr, Eid al-Adha and summer – when Lebanon fills with expat Lebanese and thousands of Arabs eager to trade the furnace of the Gulf for the cooler Med, travellers who do not book in advance will find their options severely limited.

True budget hotels don't exist, but at the more reasonable end of the market ($70-$90 a night), you'll find creaky yet charming family-run options such as Hotel Cavalier (Mohammad Abdul Baki Street, T 01 353 001) and The Mayflower (Nehme Yafet Street, T 01 340 680). In Ashrafiye, Hayete (Furn el-Hayek) is a lovely four-bedroom B&B in Mardiros Altounian's Daouk Building.

Further up the price scale is 35 Rooms (Baalbeck Street, T 01 345 676), which is pleasant and vaguely 'designy'. But then there's nothing good until the $200-plus range, with hotels like Le Vendôme (Ain el-Mreisse, T 01 369 280), luxury the Louis XVI way, and Le Bristol (Madame Curie Street, T 01 351 400), which is being overhauled. A plethora of boutique hotels are promised, but for now, global downturn and regional upheaval keep them on paper. *For full addresses, see Resources.*

Four Seasons

Next to Kohn Pedersen Fox's Marina Tower, this 25-storey hotel is a favourite of Gulf visitors. The 230 rooms each come with a terrace looking on to the city, marina, mountains or sea. The interiors are the work of Four Seasons stalwart Pierre-Yves Rochon, and might best be described as Arabasian classic with a modern twist: swirly carpets, oversized vases and Brobdingnagian floral displays with the odd glint of gold. This is changing, however, as new artwork is introduced to give the hotel a more Lebanese identity; the decor is sleekest in rooms such as the Diplomatic Suite (above). The rooftop pool is for guests only, but the terrace bar opens to all in the evening. Cocktail in hand, the view from 119m up at sunset is magical.
1418 Wafik Sinno Avenue, T 01 761 000,
www.fourseasons.com/beirut

Le Gray

In many ways, this is the hotel Beirut has been waiting for. Stylish, contemporary, sexy – a modern classic. In a prime spot on Martyrs' Square, the smooth facade could almost be French Mandate, with its ranks of tall, narrow windows and street-level sunshades. But the building, by Kevin Dash, is new, as revealed in flashes of modernity like the glass-walled rooftop bar and sixth-floor lounge (opposite), infinity pool overlooking the Mediterranean and vertiginous light well. The rooms and suites (one-bed Corner Suite, above) are understated and elegant. The furniture, decorated in Mary Fox Linton's chic palette of whites, muted greys, greens and blues, has a midcentury feel and contrasts nicely with the hotel's 500-plus pieces of modern art by the likes of Valerie Boy and Nadim Karam.
Weygand Street/Martyrs' Square, T 01 971 111, www.campbellgrayhotels.com

Phoenicia

In 1961, the Phoenicia became the first of Pan Am's InterContinental hotel chain to open outside the Americas. Designed by Edward Durell Stone, its distinctive salmon-pink facade, arabesque balconies and wraparound terrace made it an icon of the jet age. Gutted during the wars, it reopened in 2000, its midcentury charm obscured under 21st-centurion touches like Romanesque mosaics and faux-Corinthian colonnades. Fortunately, its well-deserved reputation for excellent service was upheld. The rooms are a tad 'international', but comfortable, and the Eau de Vie restaurant/bar (pictured) is a swish space. Although no longer the most interesting place to stay in town, the Phoenicia is still one of the best. *Suleiman Frangieh Boulevard, T 01 369 100, www.phoeniciabeirut.com*

Hotel Albergo

Stuffed with carpets, saddle-bag cushions, Ottoman chandeliers, antique mother-of-pearl furniture, Bedouin tchotchkes and Greco-Roman bibelots, Beirut's only true boutique hotel is part neo-orientalist wonder, part Parisian boudoir. The ideal place to indulge your *Lawrence of Arabia* fantasy, it's housed in a sandstone building tucked away on a charming street; the property's lower levels were originally a 1930s family home. Extended in a style in keeping with its original surroundings, the hotel now has 33 suites, such as the Deluxe (above); each room is uniquely and lavishly adorned. The top-floor restaurant is a popular lunch spot with politicians, and the rooftop terrace is the place to relax with a chilled glass of rosé at sunset. *Abdul Wahab el-Inglizi Street, T 01 339 797, www.albergobeirut.com*

Al Bustan

Few hotels have their own music festival, but for a month in winter, usually February, the family-owned Bustan hosts divas and dancers from all over the world. The rest of the year, it caters to those who appreciate the faintly blousy, midcentury feel of its public areas, from the fabulous blue-glass accents in the lobby lounge (above) to the tartan excesses of the Scottish Bar, itself a tribute to an earlier age. Situated on a hill some 750m above the city, the rooms come with vistas over Beirut and the sea, or over the ridge to the pine forest in the neighbouring valley. Nothing like its siblings on the coast, and downright dated in places, what Al Bustan lacks in modern sophistication it makes up for in character and fading charm.
Beyt Meri, T 04 870 400,
www.albustanhotel.com

24 HOURS

SEE THE BEST OF THE CITY IN JUST ONE DAY

Choking traffic, pavements filled with parked cars and addresses explained in terms of 'landmarks', Beirut may not seem pedestrian-friendly, but walking is the best way to feel its pulse. The climate is agreeable and the city is small enough to make strolling around it a pleasure. On foot, you'll glimpse layers of architecture, hidden gardens, and moments of beauty that make Beirut special.

It's only by getting around like this that one truly appreciates institutions such as Falafel Sahyoun (Bechara el-Khoury Street, T 01 633 188), dispenser of the world's finest fritters since 1933; Barbar (Rue Spears, T 01 379 779) and its Lebanese fast food; or delicious *manakeesh* (Lebanese pizzas) at revamped Zaatar w Zeit (Independence Boulevard, behind Sodeco Square, T 01 611 488).

Walking is also a great way to see the city's galleries. Between Saleh Barakat's Agial (63 Omar bin Abdul Aziz Street, T 01 345 213) and Galerie Janine Rubeiz (Majdalani Building, General de Gaulle Avenue, T 01 868 290), you'll cover Ras Beirut's modernist heritage. Or head to arts district Karantina for Lea Sednaoui's The Running Horse (Shukri al-Khoury Street, near Sleep Comfort, T 01 562 778), Galerie Sfeir-Semler (4th floor, Tannous Building, behind Forum de Beyrouth, T 01 566 550) and Joy Mardini's Art Factum (Rehban Street, T 01 443 263). *Zawarib Beirut*, Lebanon's A-Z, which shows the buildings Beirutis navigate by, is invaluable. *For full addresses, see Resources.*

09.00 Gruen Eatery

Founded in 2005 by Maria Ousseimi, doyenne of the Beirut Art Center (see p028), and ice-cream evangelist Nayla Audi, this kicky bistro with its 1960s vibe (Panton and Bertoia chairs, leather banquettes and Tom Dixon 'Mirror Ball' lights) is such a good match for its Gefinor Center (see p069) surroundings, you might think it's been here forever. Designed by architect Joumana Ghandour Atallah,

Gruen opens out to an alfresco area, the perfect place to enjoy its Californian fusion cuisine and Lebanese classics. It's popular for lunch, but with pancakes, waffles and large pots of French-press coffee on the menu, it's also the ideal place to linger over breakfast. If you're not careful, you won't end up hitting town at all.
Block C, Gefinor Center, Mohammad Abdul Baki Street, T 01 755 322

10.30 Downtown walk

Although severely damaged during the wars and largely restructured, Central Beirut has some attractive buildings. Most are Ottoman or French Mandate, but there are also traces of more ancient pasts: the Roman baths below the Grand Serail, or the remains of the Phoenician city, visible under architect Rafael Moneo's new souks (above). There's the Maghen Abraham Synagogue (Wadi Abu Jamil Street); the Greek Orthodox Cathedral of Saint Georges (Nejmeh Square), filled with murals; and, opposite the 1934 neo-Mamluk Municipality, the Omari Mosque (Weygand Street), a palimpsest of Beirut history that has also been temple, church and cathedral. A Heritage Trail, opening in 2012, will link all these and more, finally giving one of the world's oldest cities the recognition that it deserves.

12.00 National Museum

The 1942 neo-Pharaonic National Museum, designed by Antoine Nahas and Pierre Leprince-Ringuet, serves up 11,000 years of Lebanese history in neat, beautifully displayed chunks. Shelled, flooded and torched many times, it was completely renovated in the 1990s (the priceless exhibits were saved by the prescience of then director Emir Maurice Shehab, who had concrete frames constructed around them). Today, the well-edited selection of artefacts include Roman sarcophagi from Tyre (above), playful Eshmoun baby statues and Mamluk jewellery. Call a few days ahead and you may be able to visit the basement (as yet unfinished), which houses Phoenician humanoid sarcophagi and a painted Roman tomb. Closed Mondays. *Damascus Road/Abdallah el-Yafi, T 01 426 703, www.beirutnationalmuseum.com*

15.00 Beirut Art Center

A big, white box in an industrial location, the Beirut Art Center may not sound groundbreaking, but overnight it gave the city's ever-mutating art scene a nucleus around which to organise itself. Set up by Maria Ousseimi, Lamia Joreige and Sandra Dagher, 'because not everyone can travel to New York or Paris to see an exhibition', the adaptable space houses an auditorium, a bookshop, a café and a fledgling archive, which aims to cover all Middle Eastern artists, with photographs and video footage of their work. Previous displays have included photography by Boris Mikhailov (above left) and Abbas (above right), from Ukraine and Iran respectively. But like the furiously evolving city that surrounds it, BAC is never the same place twice.
Building 13, Street 97, Jisr el-Wati,
T 01 397 018, www.beirutartcenter.org

20.30 STAY

The Beirut outpost of Michelin-starred chef Yannick Alléno's global restaurant concept comes complete with its signature tricks: a menu of exquisitely presented classics that pay scant homage to locale; and the high-design Pastry Library, where your desserts are prepared live, open-kitchen style. But when it comes to drama of the visual kind, it's Alain Moatti's million-dollar interior that steals the show. The bar (above), suspended over the dining room, is meant to resemble the underside of a Phoenician ship. Below, the tables, arranged kissing-chair style, tread a fine line between privacy and eavesdropping, making the communal one (less popular with territorial Lebanese diners), the best place for more intimate encounters. *Beirut Souks, Fakhry Bey Street, T 01 999 757, www.yannick-alleno.com*

23.00 Music Hall

In a city now moonlighting as the Ibiza of the Middle East, you may feel compelled to end your day with a bang. There's no shortage of places to go, from throbbing rooftop megaclubs to cosy pubs and bars where dancing is encouraged. One of the more popular options, the rowdy, sit-down Music Hall, is housed in a pre-wars cinema in the basement of George Addor and Dominique Julliard's glorious 1957 commercial centre, Starco. Created by the self-styled Emperor of Nowheristan, Michel Elefteriades, the venue offers a nightly roster of cabaret and musical acts (sometimes alternative, often less usual) and, once the live performances have finished, a nightclub. It's a hangout for night owls of every age.

Starco Center, Omar Daouk Street/ Wadi Abu Jamil Street, T 03 807 555

URBAN LIFE
CAFÉS, RESTAURANTS, BARS AND NIGHTCLUBS

Explosive is the best description for Beirut's nightlife scene. Few venues have been around long enough to become institutions, and some come and go in a season. This is partly because a night out here is all about moving from place to place, sampling every one. Blame this on a culinary tradition based around mezze.

Every kind of going out involves food (very few bars serve alcohol only). The finest Lebanese cuisine is dished up in the garden restaurants of the mountain resorts, although Central Beirut's Karam (Bazerkan Street, T 01 991 222) is highly recommended. As is Al-Ajami (Rafic el-Hariri, T 01 802 260) in Ramlet el-Baida. Although often empty, its Persian-inflected take on Lebanese cookery produces some of the most delicate food in town. Similarly toothsome is Varouj (Maracha Royal Street, T 03 882 933), a tiny Armenian eatery in Borj Hammoud.

Creative and unconstrained, Beirut is the cultural heart of the region, and home to a thriving music scene producing everything from folk and funk to rap and rock. Acts such as Mashrouh Leila, Munma, Scrambled Eggs, Slutterhouse, Rayess Bek and Fareeq el-Atrash, in particular, are must-sees. Alternatively, once you get past the bouncers, in summer you can dance until dawn at open-air clubs like Skybar (BIEL, T 03 939 191) and Iris (8th floor, An-Nahar Building, Martyrs' Square, T 03 090 936).

For full addresses, see Resources.

Goutons Voir

Take an old Lebanese apartment. Add a white-walled interior with splashes of colour provided by fresh flowers. Crown with a simple menu aimed at thirtysomething Beirutis who want to eat well without spending a week's wages, and you have this dependable, light-filled restaurant, opened in 2011. For less than half the price you'll pay elsewhere, you'll get an unpretentious selection of seafood, steaks, pasta, risottos and salads. The warm goat's cheese and reimagined Niçoise salad with quail eggs and tuna are lovely; foie gras and truffles also feature. For dessert, the *pain perdu* is a treat and the strawberry-topped melted chocolate fondant is sheer decadence. There's a good selection of wines by the glass.
Abdul Wahab el-Inglizi Street/Monot Street, T 01 333 644

Sweet Tea

With its verdant walls, a design patented
by MIT-award-winning Green Studios, the
roof patio of Yannick Alléno's casual-dining
venue is a breath of fresh air, literally.
Inside, Alain Moatti's design concept, a
candy-coloured affair with padded ceiling
and marquetry floors, takes over. Come
for the crispiest croissants in the city and
mouthwatering *macarons* and madeleines.
Jewellery Souk, T 01 990 845

Chez Jean Claude

In a beautiful old home on a leafy street in Ashrafiye, this upscale bistro is just the kind of unapologetically old-school dining experience you'd expect from a master tailor who lived and worked for much of his life in Paris. In the evening, sit in the original 20-seat dining room – popularity means there's now a larger annexe (above) next door – and after a *coupe de champagne* or two, the soft lighting, jazz soundtrack and panelled windows will leave you wondering if you're looking out on Rue Cler rather than Gabriel Khabbaz. With no printed menus, the daily selection is recited by attentive staff, but you can expect bistro staples such as steak au poivre, confit de canard and lentil salad with foie gras. The desserts are made on site, and the crème brûlée is legendary.
Gabriel Khabbaz Street, T 01 328 6378

Momo at the Souks

Married to the daughter of Franco-Lebanese architect and designer Annabel Karim Kassar (whose hand is visible in the mix of antique, retro and modern pieces, and cross-cultural fabrics and wall coverings), it's surprising that it took Mourad Mazouz so long to open in Beirut. Picking up where his Heddon Street, London, premises left off, this eaterie encompasses restaurant, bar and garden terrace (above), complete with loungers and rattan chairs. The clientele ranges from hip(ish) twentysomethings in the lounge to a slightly older crowd in the restaurant. Foodwise, the starters are a hybrid of North African and French dishes, such as chicken livers with hummus, and the mains tend to fall into one camp or the other; tajines or bouillabaise, for instance.
7 Jewellery Souk, T 01 999 767

Tawlet

Tucked down a cul-de-sac at the less trendy end of Mar Mikhayel, this light, airy restaurant has been the toast of the international press since it opened in 2009. An outgrowth of the farmers' market held on Saturday mornings in Central Beirut (check www.soukeltayeb. com for the location), Tawlet operates on a buffet basis. Each day a different cook contributes specialities from their village, often using produce grown in their own garden. The first eatery to capitalise on Lebanon's varied culinary traditions, Tawlet introduces foreign visitors to food they're unlikely to taste elsewhere, and young urbanites to country dishes. Open Monday to Friday for lunch and afternoon tea; Saturday for brunch, noon-4pm.
Opposite Spoiler Center, Nahr Street, T 01 448 129, www.soukeltayeb.com

St Elmo's Seaside Brasserie

This New England-style brasserie is nestled beneath the glittering buildings lining the new marina towards the St Georges (see p014) end of Zaitunay Bay. It's a nice enough place to dine or have brunch on a Sunday, but with its quayside tables and generous approach to cocktails it's a magnificent spot to sit and get pleasantly plastered while you watch the sun set over the superyachts moored in front of

you. Part of a Steven Holl-designed development set for completion in late 2012, Zaitunay Bay is to include a private members' club and a cluster of million-dollar studios. Backed on to what will eventually be a seafront park, free for mere mortals to use, the marina will be topped by an undulating green roof.
*Zaitunay Bay, T 71 712 244,
www.stelmosbrasserie.com*

Ginette

Located on the ground floor of a new-build residential tower, the spare, concrete-and-glass Ginette is the work of Räed Abillama Architects. The boutique at the rear stocks an interesting selection of clothes and accessories, and the mezzanine displays artwork courtesy of the Japanese gallery Nanzuka, which Ginette represents. Call it a concept store with a café, or a café with a concept store, Ginette is an excellent place for a salad or an open sandwich; desserts are by Nayla Audi. Breakfast on the patio, whether you plump for waffles with strawberries, or some traditional Lebanese yogurt, crispbread, *za'atar* and olives, is a great way to kickstart your morning.
Gouraud Street, T 01 570 440,
www.ginette-beirut.com

L'Humeur du Chef

Less is more. The maxim may as well be carved above the door of chef Jad el-Hage's small restaurant, situated on a side street in Mar Mikhayel. The kitchen is so open that you eat in it, or rather beside it, on high chairs at a long communal table flanking the action. Not only can you watch your meal being prepared, you have the chance to get to know el-Hage, a former hotelier and restaurant manager, who is happy to chat as he cooks. As the name suggests, the restaurant isn't about choice. You're guaranteed a starter, a salad and a main (depending on what catches chef's eye at the morning market), and a dessert. If you're lucky, this will be a generous helping of the house's to-die-for chocolate mousse.
Azirian Building, Ibn el-Rabih Street,
T 03 354 149

Al-Mayass

An early offerer of Armenian cuisine (trendy in Beirut these days), Mayass is housed in what could be a 1970s Italian restaurant. There's even a guitarist some nights, who looks as if he's about to burst into a rendition of 'Volare'. Don't let the kitsch deflect you. This family-run venue is a class act and the food is pure magic. True, the menu resembles that of most Armenian eateries, and also includes a number of Lebanese offerings such as hummus and tabbouleh, but the finesse with which everything is prepared can be tasted in every bite. The unmissables? The *makanek* (mini-sausages) in pomegranate syrup, the succulent kebabs in black cherry sauce, and, of course, the meat *mante*, a kind of baked ravioli, served in a citrusy, sumac-sprinkled yogurt sauce. *Trabaud Street, Furn el-Hayek, T 01 215 046*

Burgundy
An unassuming exterior belies this eaterie's semi-brutal interior, designed by Riad Kamel, with retro-futuristic chandeliers by PSLAB. The cellar is full of hard-to-find vintages, and the menu is equally considered, from the foie gras to the cedar-smoked Wagyu beef, all lovingly presented by Canadian Brody White, who trained under Joël Robuchon. *752 Gouraud Street, T 01 999 820*

Abdel Wahab

Perhaps a tad 'Ye Olde Oriente' for modern palates, Abdel Wahab, in business since 1999, is proof that when done properly, traditional can outdo contemporary. The food is no-nonsense Lebanese: hot and cold mezze, grilled meats and fruit-tastic dessert. There are more kinds of hummus than you'll know what to do with, as well as *mouhammara* (a spicy walnut dip), salads, and hot dishes such as the tongue-twisting *rqaeq* (deep-fried, crispy cheese rolls) and *sojouk* (spicy sausage). Meats range from assorted kebabs and chicken brochettes to quail. Weather permitting (at least nine months out of 12), the best tables are on the buzzy rooftop, where your view of other diners, many smoking *arguileh* (hookahs), will compensate for the lack of anything more panoramic.
Abdul Wahab el-Inglizi Street, T 01 200 550

Torino

Easily identified by the neon sign in its window, above owner/DJ and bon viveur Andreas Bulos' turntable, this tiny café/bar (emphasis on bar) was the place that started the ball rolling in Gemmayze. Housed in a single sandstone vault, and visually a mix of fabrics, wooden seating and plastic-fantastic touches from the 1970s, it serves by day as a hangout for local hipsters, jobbing journalists on the lam and other charming reprobates who hew to the maxim that if cocktails aren't appropriate before six, there's nothing wrong with a shot of brandy in your *doppio* before then. After dark, the music gets louder and the macchiatos and correttos give way to cocktails and shots. When things get tight inside, the crowd spills on to the pavement to keep the evening going.
Gouraud Street

Cro Magnon

Brainchild of restaurateur Joey Ghazal, who cut his teeth in Montreal before returning to Lebanon in 2010, Cro Magnon's mahogany panelling, vaulted copper ceiling and potted palms could be straight out of 1930s Chicago. Adding to the Capone-esque vibe, there's a private dining room and a cigar lounge, which may or may not survive the introduction of anti-smoking laws in 2012. This is probably the only restaurant in the Middle East with an in-house butcher, whose cuts can be bought at the glass counter by the entrance. From sirloin to filet mignon, Cro Magnon is carnivorous but not exclusively about beef. Veal, lamb and seafood are also available. Vegetarians may even be able to make a meal out of the side orders.
Zaitunay Bay, T 01 370 356,
www.lecromagnon.com

Democratic Republic of Music

Although it's also a restaurant, the main reason to visit Ghazi Abdel Baki's DRM is for the live performances by local, regional and international artists in a space that's intimate without feeling cramped. Mainly known for its alternative and acoustic roster, the venue also dabbles with events of other kinds, such as Wicked Kitchen, a live cooking/DJ happening dreamed up by the team behind Amsterdam's Supperclub. DRM's raw and industrial multi-level concert space is in the basement, and is where local record label Forward Music hosts gigs. As you might expect, the acoustics throughout are pitch-perfect, so even when the crowd gets rowdy, amplifiers don't require ramping up to compensate.
Sourati Street, T 01 752 202,
www.drmlebanon.com

Chez Sami

Fish, Lebanese-style, is fresh and mostly fried (though it can be barbecued or baked). It's served, head and all, with lemon and a creamy, tahini sauce called *taratour*; or perhaps as *siyadiyeh*, a blend of flaked fish, toasted almonds and spiced rice; or *samkeh harra*, chunks of white fish in a spicy sauce. Then there's fish as mezze: sardines, whitebait, calamari and *kibbet samak*, the seafood take on lamb and bulgar-wheat balls. Chez Sami has all these, and diners can select the fish, lobster, langoustine or crab that most appeals. Set in an old home about 20km north-east of Beirut, its terraces overlook Jounieh Bay. Come here for Sunday lunch and you may well stay, drinking *arak* until past sundown. *Jounieh Old Road, Maameltein, T 09 646 064*

Marinella

Don't let the cool grey-and-white interior fool you — the menu at Sophie Shoucair's Marinella is a feast for the senses. The trattoria's short menu varies from week to week, although some favourites, such as the gnocchi in creamy lemon sauce, and *risotto al funghi*, have so far remained constants. With a pitch-perfect location, across the road from car repair shops and garages, and limited seating, the restaurant fills up fast, especially as it has developed a loyal following since its launch in 2011. It's also an easy place for single diners, who can sit at the front counter. Marinella is currently open for lunch only, which is a good thing. Were it also open in the evenings, the temptation to eat here twice a day might prove impossible to resist. Closed Sundays.
Madrid Street, T 01 442 342

Casablanca

Quirky, art-strewn and all-organic, Casablanca occupies the top floor of an Ottoman villa overlooking the Corniche (see p089). The East-meets-West food, though, is far from antique. Many dishes, such as the rice-paper wraps or bento boxes, are overtly Asian, whereas others, like the steamed sea bass with ginger, are given a delicate Asian twist. It's a popular spot for Sunday brunch, when coffee and eggs Benedict at a table with a sea view is a fine way to recover from the excesses of the night before. When crowded, the place can be noisy, and prices are more boutique than bargain (it's easy to pay $50 a head without alcohol), but almost two decades old and still going strong, Casablanca is a Beiruti institution. *Kaddoura Building, Dar el-Mreisse Street, T 01 369 334*

INSIDER'S GUIDE

LARA KHOURY, FASHION DESIGNER

A beneficiary of STARCH (see p084), Beirut's start-up foundation for young fashion designers, ESMOD Paris graduate Lara Khoury creates clothes that are on the conceptual side of wearable. From her Gemmayze atelier she produces two women's collections each year, which she sells online through www.notjustalabel.com.

To get her fix of art and design, Khoury likes Smogallery (Dagher Building, 77 Senegal Street, T 01 572 202), Gregory Gatserelia's garage-turned-gallery, and Over the Counter (Saint Antoine Building, 150 Abdul Wahab el-Inglizi Street, T 01 322 841), a vintner that doubles as a design space, which has 'the best accessories in town'. For furniture of her own, she raids the packed warehouses of Basta, uncovering everything from 1970s sofas and art deco dining tables to 17th-century mother-of-pearl wardrobes.

When going out, Lara stays local. If unwinding after work or meeting friends, she heads to Kayan (Lebanon Street, T 01 563 611), a cosy and welcoming bar/eaterie. Later, she may move on to Dictateur (30 Badawi Street, behind Al-Mandaloun, T 70 451 512), a busy bar with a courtyard garden, or Art Lounge (Naggiar Building, next to Karantina Bridge, Corniche al-Nahr, T 03 997 676), for its exhibitions and performances. When she wants something less frenetic, Gou (St Nicholas Street, T 01 200 765), a modern café/restaurant, serves the best hot chocolate in town.
For full addresses, see Resources.

ARCHITOUR
A GUIDE TO BEIRUT'S ICONIC BUILDINGS

From the 1920s on, Beirut began to experiment with contemporary architecture. Some buildings, such as Antoine Tabet's 1938 Collège de la Sagesse (Mar Mitr Road) and Farid Trad's 1947 UNESCO Palace (Bir Hassan, T 01 850 013) remain, but most survivors date from the 1950s and 1960s, when the city fell in love with modernism.

Unfortunately, post-wars building booms levelled many of the best examples. André Leconte's 1955 airport and Adib, Makdisse and Schayer's 1957 Carlton Hotel are two of the most egregious losses. Others barely survive. Along General de Gaulle Avenue, Joseph Philippe Karam's Immeuble Shams, and Schayer and Adib's Shell Building have, with cruel irony, been 'modernised' with superfluous elements. In Hamra, seek out the 1971 Near East School of Theology (Jeanne d'Arc Street) and Alvar Aalto and Alfred Roth's complex, now the Fransabank Center (Hamra Street).

Not all the best architecture is yesterday's. Yves Lion and Claire Piguet's French Embassy (Rue de Damas) opened in 1997, and Kevin Dash's Bank Audi HQ (Bab Idriss) in 2002. Nabil Gholam's beautifully lit 2010 Platinum Tower anchors Steven Holl's new marina. More is coming. Arata Isozaki's Beirut Gardens, Norman Foster's 3Beirut and Herzog & de Meuron's Beirut Terraces are due by 2014. Further off, there's Renzo Piano's city museum, Jean Nouvel's Landmark tower and a vast retail hub by Zaha Hadid. *For full addresses, see Resources.*

Université Saint Joseph

Youssef Tohme's USJ campus extension, undertaken in collaboration with local practice 109 Architects, is one of Beirut's best examples of urban planning on a public project. A series of buildings, including sports facilities, administrative spaces and lecture halls, it was imagined as a single mass. Out of this, the component structures were to be carved, so that while each building would be distinct, when viewed as a whole the voids would present as integral spaces. Clad in a combination of polycarbon panelling and variegated, tawny sandstone, the complex is punctured by glass walls, and windows and doors are arranged in an intricate pattern. It gives the impression that when Tohme sat down and decided to sculpt stone, he decided to sculpt space as well.
Damascus Road/Corniche Pierre Gemayel

Sursock Palace

Finished in 1860 and located on a tree-lined street beside the Greek Orthodox Archdiocese and Saint Nicholas Steps, the former residence of Moussa Sursock, scion of a wealthy property-owning family, is one of the last city palaces still inhabited by its original owners. Home to Lady Yvonne Cochrane, daughter of Alfred Sursock, and her third son and his family, it's a charming example of the almost confectionery mix of Levantine, Venetian and Ottoman influences popular at the time. Two more family residences are nearby. Next door to the bold yellow Linda Sursock Palace is the white Nicolas Sursock Palace – a modern-art gallery since 1961 (due to reopen after renovations in mid 2013). *Rue Sursock, T 01 218 720, www.sursockpalace.com*

062

Interdesign Building

Visually about halfway between a *Transformers* toy and a set of high-end concept speakers, Khalil and Georges Khoury's graceful concrete-and-glass hulk of a building serves as the headquarters of the family's less daring furniture chain, Interdesign. Assistants to Michel Ecochard, the French architect who drew up a never-realised urban plan for Beirut in 1955, the brothers designed the building in the early 1970s. Work began shortly afterwards but was halted by the turbulent events of the next two decades. Finally finished in 1996, the structure is so magnificently at odds with its surroundings that it looks as if it has just landed, and presents the city with every bit as much of an architectural challenge today as it did when it was first drawn up.

95 Rome Street, www.interdesign.com.lb

The Egg

Designed in 1965 by Joseph Philippe Karam, this curious structure is all that remains of the Beirut City Center, a five-level subterranean mall, topped by a slender slab of concrete on which a cinema and two soaring office towers were to be perched. Never finished, the substructure and heavily scarred concrete bubble housing the cinema, which until recently still contained a few blasted ranks of orange plastic chairs, are all that remains. An increasingly rare example of Lebanon's modernist love affair, the Egg, as it's known, is part of the controversy about the city's disappearing architectural heritage. Repeatedly (but erroneously) claimed as being under threat, it is to be preserved and incorporated into Christian de Portzamparc's tower complex on the site. *Gellas Street/Bechara el-Khoury Street*

Khashoggi Mosque

A total contrast in both style and intent to the soaring, anachronistic Mohammad al-Amin (see p009), this gracious mosque, which faces the southern end of Beirut's biggest park, the pine-forested Horsh Beirut, is unassuming by today's supersized standards. Designed by Assem Salam, a descendant of a notable Beiruti political family, the mosque's stylised crowns, slender cupola and spacious, low-slung prayer hall meld past and present. With its masterful use of concrete and sandstone features, Khashoggi was considered a landmark in contemporary Islamic architecture when completed in 1968. It still is. Simple, graceful, verging on abstract, Salam's mosque is a reminder of a time in Lebanon when modernity and religion were not considered incompatible. *Jalloul*

Barakat Building
Designed by Youssef Afandi Aftimos,
and finished in 1936, this neo-Ottoman-
style sandstone building was one of the
first in the city to use concrete in its
construction. Bullet-riddled, it is being
partially restored. After the insertion
of a modern core, by architect Youssef
Haidar, it will reopen in 2013 as a cultural
centre and museum of urban life.
Elias Sarkis Avenue/Damascus Road

الإمتداد
٣

Electricité du Liban Building

Inspired by Brazilian modernism, Pierre Neema's exquisitely proportioned 1966 HQ for Lebanon's erratic electricity provider is (ironically) a blazing beacon of light by night. One of the country's lesser-known architects, Neema also designed the 1963 Maison de l'Artisan, a glass-and-concrete pavilion on the Corniche (see p089), which was bastardised beyond all recognition post-wars. The EDL building has fared better. Although the midcentury fixtures and furnishings have gone, its exterior has survived. Home to what was probably Lebanon's first green rooftop, which extends at plaza level above the reception, this dynamic slender slab, with its delicate concrete sunscreen facade, still impresses despite decades of semi-neglect.
Nahr Street

Gefinor Center

'Say "take me to Gefinor" to any Beirut resident,' the *International Herald Tribune* gushed in the early 1970s, 'and he'll have no trouble finding the elegant skyscraper.' Designed by Austrian architect Victor Gruen, the man who gave the world the shopping mall, this hunk of black-glass-and-steel midcentury sexiness was dubbed a Wall Street in miniature, and was Beirut's most modern business destination at the time. Broken into five blocks, the tallest of which is 20 storeys, Gefinor seems wasted on offices. In a more perfect world, its tree-lined plaza, underground parking, atrium shopping spaces and touches like the suspended staircase sweeping down from Block D would catch a developer's eye and be transformed into a boutique hotel and high-end residential complex.
Mohammad Abdul Baki Street

Notre Dame du Liban, Harissa
Built between 1969 and 1993, the late
Pierre el-Khoury's cathedral for the
Maronite Catholic church sits 650m
above the Bay of Jounieh. The basilica
was conceived as a series of sculptural
concrete ribs, set in five tilting shells that
rise from the narthex to the glass apse.
Homage is paid to traditional Levantine
religious architecture in the sandstone
walls below the raw-concrete shell.

SHOPPING

THE BEST RETAIL THERAPY AND WHAT TO BUY

Shopping has always been one of Beirut's raisons d'être – for centuries, it was the port that served Syria and Iraq. Compared to the Gulf's instant cities, it has fewer global brands, though Aïshti (71 Rue Moutran, T 01 991 111) is gilding the centre with luxury designer labels, but it more than compensates with local talent.

Light on markets, Beirut is about the boutique. Concept stores, like Plum (Berytus Building, Park Avenue, T 01 976 566) and Piaff (Maktabi Building, Clemenceau Street, T 01 362 368), stock an international mix, while Lebanese designers, from Elie Saab (Bab Idriss, opposite Starco Center, T 01 981 982) to Krikor Jabotian (Dakdouk Building, Salim Bustros Street, T 01 204 793), abound.

Jewellery is a good buy, particularly at Selim Mouzannar (82 Shehade Street, T 01 331 299), with its line by Ranya Sarakbi. For contemporary home furnishings, there's Chakib Richani (George Haddad Street, T 01 973 088). Iwan Maktabi (Quantum Building, Charles Malek Avenue, T 01 336 301) deals in carpets and calligraphy, and 44 Souk an-Najjarine (Said Akel Street, T 01 998 822) is good for other antiques. Inaash (Bikhazi & Charif Building, behind Sidani Street, T 01 740 609) sells delicate embroidery made by Palestinian refugees. Handmade chocolates can be found at Noura (Sassine Square, T 01 337 599), and boxes of baklava are best picked up at Amal Bohsali (Alfred Nobel Street, T 01 354 400). *For full addresses, see Resources.*

Maison Rabih Kayrouz

As you walk down the short flight of stairs into Rabih Kayrouz's boutique – a giant walk-in closet-like premises, co-designed by Karen Chekerdjian (see p083) – you momentarily become the centre of attention. Enjoy it, for it doesn't last. Once you're inside, Kayrouz's clothes take centre stage. Sensual yet cerebral, they exude the glamour of a more formal era without compromising their modernity.

Whether creating couture or prêt-à-porter, Kayrouz applies the craftsmanship of the former to the mass sensibility of the latter, and has gained a reputation as the fastest rising star in Lebanon's design pantheon. But with a boutique in Paris and shows during that city's Fashion Week, that accolade may already be dated.
Darwish Haddad Street, T 01 444 221, www.maisonrabihkayrouz.com

Studio Karim Bekdache

An inveterate collector of cast-offs,
architect Karim Bekdache has spent the
better part of two decades picking his way
through Lebanese homes, thrift stores
and even the occasional dumpster, to
accumulate period Lebanese furnishings
from the 1950s to 1970s. Bekdache was
brought up in a Raoushe apartment block
where, for a while, his grandfather, Nadim
Majdalani, ran an atelier with cult French
designer Jean Royère. His collection
includes some imports but is mostly local,
serving as a reminder of Beirut's pre-
wars adoration for all that was midcentury
and modern. The biggest draw, however,
may be the banged-up signs, billboards
and illuminated hoardings rescued from
cinemas, shops and garages all over town.
*Kassab Building, Madrid Street,
T 01 566 323, www.karimbekdache.com*

Orient 499

In a city suddenly awash with handicraft shops, Frank Luca and Aida Kawas' spacious boutique in the shadow of the old Holiday Inn showcases some of the region's best products. Both shop and atelier (many of the items on sale have been specially commissioned by the duo), it offers a broad range, from delicately embroidered shirts and flowing abaya-style gowns, to mother-of-pearl inlay furniture, finely etched brassware, olive-oil soaps, antique fabrics, jewellery and even calligraphic art pieces. Products are traditional but with a contemporary edge, and the collection concentrates mainly on objects made in Lebanon and Syria; some, notably the fabrics and bedspreads, are from Egypt, Central Asia and India.
499 Omar Daouk Street, T 01 369 499, www.orient499.com

Johnny Farah

Food activist, chef and restaurateur – he co-owns Casablanca (see p053) – Johnny Farah also creates a tasteful range of leather goods. A mechanical engineer by training, Farah developed an interest in Scandinavian design, and attributes his passion for leather craftwork to meetings with Arne Jacobsen and Hans Wegner. His hides are vegetable-tanned, making them almost as soft and supple as living skin, and fastenings and other hardware are made from hand-moulded brass. The collection is divided between a partly machine-made eponymous range, and the JF 37 37 line, which is cut and sewn by hand. As well as belts, wallets and bags, Farah produces covetable totes, attaché cases, and slip-on shoes and lace-ups.
Said Akel Street, T 01 974 808, www.johnnyfarah.com

Bokja

Were there to be a riot in a sweet shop, the fallout may resemble Hoda Baroudi and Maria Hibri's acid-coloured atelier. Lime-green and neon-orange walls serve as the backdrop to an array of recycled, technicoloured furniture, given new life through being reupholstered in a variety of fabrics. Art deco loungers, Louis XVI sofas and Scandinavian Modern armchairs are reimagined using old Bedouin dresses, Bukharian silk tapestries, ikat from Uzbekistan, kitsch Chinese synthetics, and 1960s geometric prints, leavened with gentle bursts of pop art embroidery created in-house. A little bit Lacroix, a little bit LSD, this is furniture with character and not for the faint of heart.
Building 332, Mukhalissiye Street,
T 01 975 576, www.bokjadesign.com

Nada Debs

The cosmopolitan feel of Nada Debs' design is born of her quest to marry two aesthetic cultures: the decorative geometries of the Middle East and the austere rationality of Japan, where Debs grew up. Some items fall more into one camp than the other, but most mix both. The range of homewares and furniture, such as the natural walnut with mother-of-pearl inlay table (above), are linked by an appreciation for pattern, which Debs channels using oversized arabesques, abstract chinoiserie and simple geometric forms. As much at home worked in wood and metal as Plexiglas, her creations are the logical continuation of the once flourishing connection between the Middle and the Far East.

Building E-332, Mukhalissiye Street, T 01 999 002, www.nadadebs.com

XXieme Siècle

You can thank Souheil Hanna's grandmother for this cool wonderland of midcentury furniture and furnishings, so well laid out it's practically *prêt-à-habiter*. Or rather you can thank her console – a Jean Royère – which first caught Hanna's magpie eye and kicked off his passion for collecting pieces from this period. Fast-forward a decade or so, and the fruits of his labours can be found at the showroom he runs with his sister, Hala. The stock spans from furniture, floor coverings and light fixtures to mobiles, ashtrays and op art. A liberal sprinkling of names – Calder, Colombo, Ponti, Vasarely – is mixed with items by modern Lebanese designers, busy building reputations of their own. *Hanna Residential Building, Abdel Aal Street/Makdisi Street, T 01 742 020, www.xxesieclegalerie.com*

Karen Chekerdjian

Housed in a vaulted mezzanine space off the main road ringing Beirut's port, the metal warehouse-turned-boutique of interior and product designer Karen Chekerdjian stocks a complete collection of her furniture and homewares. Much of Chekerdjian's work is inspired by vintage objects (the metal vats once used by iced-sherbet vendors; wire-mesh pantry cabinets), or it draws on traditional techniques of craftsmanship. The results, however, are clearly contemporary. Chekerdjian runs the boutique under the generous rubric of 'things we make and things we like', and the store also stocks a selection of slow-food products, and handmade pieces by other designers that are complementary to her vision. *Darwish Haddad Street, T 01 570 572, www.karenchekerdjian.com*

STARCH

Founded in 2008 by Rabih Kayrouz (see
p073), local mover-and-shaker Tala Hajjar,
and Solidere, the company rebuilding the
city centre, the STARCH Foundation selects
a clutch of promising young designers
each year and takes them under its wing.
Helping them to develop their collections
and communication skills, it sells their
work here at its eponymous boutique.
Said Akel Street, www.starchfoundation.org

Papercup

A labour of love, Rania Naufal's small but perfectly put together bookstore not only offers one of the finest selections of magazines in the country, it presents a well-chosen range of books on design, architecture and art (it was once the only place in the Middle East you were likely to find a copy of *Tom of Finland XXL*), as well as a leftfield assortment of illustrated novels and books about Beirut. An early outpost in the rapidly gentrifying Mar Mikhayel district, and host of the occasional reading or talk, it occupies a space that is part bookstore and part community centre. Papercup also serves coffee, tea and homemade cake – fine reasons, if any were needed, to linger a bit longer. Closed on Sundays.
*Agopian Building, Pharoun Street,
T 01 443 083, www.papercupstore.com*

Senteurs d'Orient

This modern reworking of the millennia-old Levantine tradition of soap-making began with the production of hand soaps and bath bars, but has expanded into essential oils, bath salts and liquid soaps. Based on shea butter, rather than olive oil, the Senteurs range is additive-free and utilises natural ingredients. Tastefully packaged, its bath bars come carved in graceful arabesques, and the liquid soap range is best dispensed in the locally handblown glass bottles. Senteurs d'Orient has taken the fragrances of the Middle East – orange blossom, almond, laurel, lavender, cedar, olive and honey – and infused them into products so gentle you won't need to moisturise, and so fragrant, you'll smell good enough to eat. *Block A, Gefinor Center, Clemenceau Street, T 01 744 762, www.senteursdorient.com*

SPORTS AND SPAS
WORK OUT, CHILL OUT OR JUST WATCH

Beirut isn't the best city for sports. The huge Camille Chamoun Stadium (Salim Salam, T 01 842 212), destroyed by the Israelis in 1982 and rebuilt for the 2000 AFC Asian Cup, is rarely used. Football and basketball are popular, but occasional clashes between supporters keep most spectators at home. There is horse racing at the Hippodrome du Parc de Beyrouth (Abdallah el-Yafi, T 01 632 515) but, built in 1885, the racecourse has seen better days.

Gyms and pools are plentiful but most are members only. Out of town, the options are better. Beach-going is a national pastime and the coastline offers much for swimmers; sunken archaeological sites and shipwrecks draw divers. The mountains provide caving, paragliding, climbing and more. The Lebanon Mountain Trail (www.lebanontrail.org) runs 440km from Qobaiyat to Marjayoun; maps and local guides are available. In winter, there's skiing, snowboarding and snowshoeing (www.skileb.com), and in spring, white-water rafting on the Assi and Litani (www.assirafting.com). Limited infrastructure and dangers like unexploded ordnance make it advisable to join excursions led by knowledgeable local operators, such as Vamos Todos (www.vamos-todos.com).

Finally, for the competitive, there's the Rally of Lebanon every September, the Beirut Marathon in November, and the Mountain to Sea Challenge, a race due to be run for the first time in 2012. *For full addresses, see Resources.*

Corniche

One of the city's few open public spaces and a de rigueur destination for foreign journalists, all of whom conjure the same astonishment at the sight of 'women wearing hijabs walking next to women in shorts', Beirut's 4.5km seafront Corniche is a favoured place for outdoor pursuits other than casual orientalism. For some, this means an *arguileh*, a deckchair, a pair of sunglasses and a bit of Arab pop, but the broad seaside pavement also attracts strollers and joggers, especially in the early morning and around sunset. The terrain here is paving slabs, rather than a track, but it's nothing that a decent pair of shoes can't handle. At the weekend, runners share the Corniche's salt air and spectacular views with rollerbladers, skateboarders and the odd Sunday cyclist.
Raoushe to Ain el-Mreisse

American University of Beirut pool
Part of the sports complex designed by
VJAA for Beirut's oldest university, the
Charles W Hostler Center is geothermally
cooled by seawater piped from across
the road. To keep energy costs down, it
was positioned to benefit from prevailing
winds and shading. The glass walls of the
25m indoor pool overlook the Med; time
it right, and you'll swim into the sunset.
Charles W Hostler Center, T 01 350 000

Faraya Mzaar and Faqra

Essentially a coastal strip and a high-altitude valley wedged between two mountain ranges, Lebanon's dramatic topography ensures two constants: visual glamour and a generous annual blanketing of powdery snow. An hour out of town — 40 minutes if you drive the Lebanese way — Faraya Mzaar is home to the country's best ski resorts. Popular with wealthy Beirutis, who keep gazillion-dollar chalets in neighbouring Faqra, its slopes run from 1,870m to 2,300m. Although not the most challenging in the world, they come with sensational sea views. Raucous après-ski, some fine dining (yes, Le 1700, we mean you; T 03 441 700), and cosy auberges, like the sophisticated URBAN (above and opposite; T 09 341 541), provide the perfect excuse not to head back to Beirut.

Golf Club of Lebanon
What Beirut's only 18-hole championship
course lacks in flash, it more than makes
up for in pedigree. On the fringes of
the city when it opened in 1923, and
still located in a green, rolling area that
was mostly pine forests and sand dunes
until well into the 1970s, the club now
finds itself in the heart of the bustling
southern suburbs. Invisible from the road,
the par 71 course – an improbable oasis
of green that is now tightly hemmed in
by housing on every side – materialises
abruptly from the air on some of the
flights touching down at nearby Beirut
International Airport. The club welcomes
visiting golfers and also has a 33m
outdoor pool with six lanes, excellent
tennis courts (both clay and hardcourt),
squash courts and a small gym.
*Abbas el-Mousawwi Street, Bir Hassan,
Ouzai, T 01 826 335, www.golfclub.org.lb*

ESCAPES

WHERE TO GO IF YOU WANT TO LEAVE TOWN

For a country the size of a postage stamp, Lebanon has much to offer. Popular summer choices are the mountains or the Med, where private beach clubs reign. The best are Jiyyeh's Lazy B (see p102) and Bamboo Bay (T 07 995 045), Eddé Sands (T 09 546 666) or White Beach (06 742 404) in Jbeil and Batroun respectively.

The lower temperatures and views in mountain towns such as Broumana and Beyt Meri make them ideal for long lunches. Mounir (Camille Chamoun Boulevard, T 04 873 900) in Broumana, and Restaurant Fadel (T 04 980 979) and Locanda Corsini (T 04 982 689) in Naas, are lovely. For setting alone, visit Mir Amin (T 70 103 222), a hotel/restaurant in an early 19th-century Italo-Levantine palace in the Shouf. About 40km south of Beirut, Sidon's warren of an old city is a gem, packed with trading houses, souks and crumbling hammams. The restored 18th-century Debbane Palace (Al-Moutran Street, T 07 720 110) has a beautiful interior.

One of three places vying for title of oldest continually inhabited city (the others are Jericho and Damascus), Byblos can boast beaches and charming (if touristy) souks. Dine at Bab al-Mina (Byblos Port, T 09 540 475) or Hotel Byblos-sur-Mer's seafood eaterie, Dar l'Azrak (Old Port, Jbeil, T 09 737 379). Of the latter's two spaces, one has a glass floor revealing the Greek and Roman remains beneath. It's fine, but head to the summer annexe instead. *For full addresses, see Resources.*

Ixsir, Basbina

One of 40 or so wineries in the country (Massaya, Ksara and Kefraya in the Bekaa Valley are also notable), Ixsir is set in the hills of Basbina, 50km north of the capital. Making wines from grapes grown at different Lebanese locations, including a plot beside the Roman temple in Niha, Ixsir is housed in concrete premises sunk beneath a 17th-century sandstone house that serves as gateway to the winery below.

Lit by skylights, which flood even the lowest levels with daylight, the gentle rampways, barrel vaults, fermentation chambers and offices are the work of Raëd Abillama Architects, and have been picking up plaudits, including a 2011 Good Green Design Award. One of Ixsir's major shareholders is Brazilian-Lebanese motor mogul Carlos Ghosn. *T 09 210 023, www.ixsir.com.lb*

Rachid Karami International Fair

That Oscar Niemeyer's partially finished International Fair in Tripoli still impresses is testament to the power of his vision. The city was occupied in 1976 by the Syrian army, and the Fair looted and razed, before it was returned to Lebanese control 18 years later. Today, the collection of elegant shells is best viewed from the panoramic eaterie at the top of the cylindrical water tower. From here, look out over the monumental arch, the dome of the experimental theatre and the graceful pointed arches of the Lebanese pavilion (above), towards the lily-shaped helipad, the concrete-and-glass exhibition halls, and the low-slung gateway and concrete canopy framing the entrance. Each of Niemeyer's buildings is so delicate, it looks as if it might float away in a stiff breeze. *Al-Mina, Tripoli, www.lebanon-fair.com*

Baalbek

The stunning temple complex at Baalbek, about 90km east of Beirut, was the centrepiece of the Roman colony of Heliopolis, which had more inhabitants in 20BC than the town does today. It was composed of two main temples, one dedicated to Jupiter and one to Bacchus, god of wine. Built in Phoenician times, Jupiter was the biggest temple the Romans ever built. Its 54 columns were 20m tall; today, only six survive on site. Bacchus (pictured), notorious location of sacred orgies, has fared better. Apart from the roof and a few toppled columns, it's mostly intact. Larger than the Parthenon and elaborately carved and decorated, its walls bear traces of the names of 18th- and 19th-century visitors, including Kaiser Wilhelm II, who paid for the complex to be excavated. Open 9am to 5-6pm.

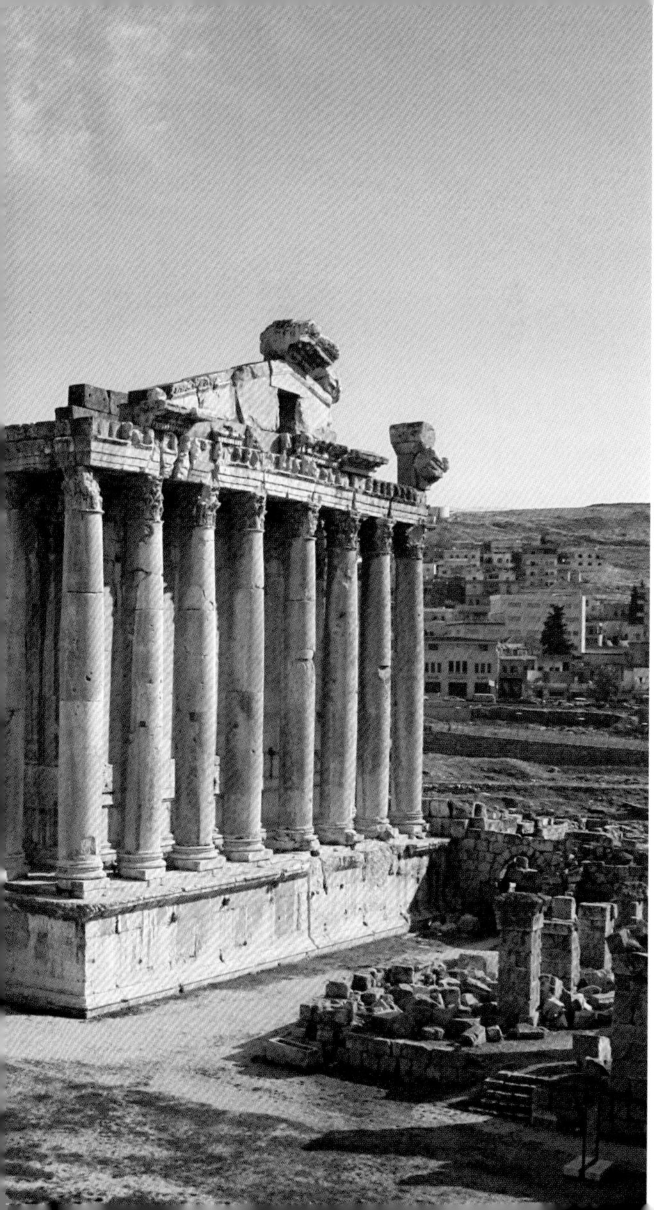

Lazy B, Jiyyeh

Beirut's one useable beach, Ramlet el-Baida, is too 'popular' for many locals, so come the weekend, half the city heads out of town. They'll either make for the coast at Batroun or Byblos, 30 and 40 minutes respectively by car; or head south to the cluster of lush beach clubs on Jiyyeh Bay, where the sands may hide the lost Roman town of Porphyrion. This being Lebanon, going to the seaside is less about getting wet than getting a tan and socialising. All beach clubs have sea access, of course, but between the pools, bars, restaurants, hairdressers and mani/pedi salons (so you don't need to go home before going out), and after-dark parties (if you prefer to remain), actually getting into the Mediterranean may prove more difficult than you would imagine.
T 70 950 010, www.lazyb.me

NOTES
SKETCHES AND MEMOS

RESOURCES

CITY GUIDE DIRECTORY

A

Abdel Wahab 046
Abdul Wahab el-Inglizi Street
T 01 200 550
www.ghiaholding.com

Abed Clocktower 010
Nejmeh Square

Agial Art Gallery 024
63 Omar bin Abdul Aziz Street
T 01 345 213

Aïshti 072
71 Rue Moutran
T 01 991 111
www.aishti.com

Al-Ajami 032
Rafic el-Hariri
T 01 802 260

Amal Bohsali 072
Alfred Nobel Street
T 01 354 400
www.abohsali.com.lb

**American University of
Beirut pool** 090
Charles W Hostler Center
American University of Beirut
T 01 350 000
www.aub.edu.lb

Art Factum Gallery 024
Rehban Street
T 01 443 263
www.artfactumgallery.com

Art Lounge 054
Naggiar Building
Next to Karantina Bridge
Corniche al-Nahr
T 03 997 676
www.artlounge.net

B

Bab al-Mina 096
Byblos Port
T 09 540 475
www.babelmina.com

Bamboo Bay 096
Jiyyeh
T 07 995 045
www.bamboo-bay.com

Bank Audi HQ 056
Bab Idriss

Barakat Building 066
Elias Sarkis Avenue/Damascus Road
www.beitbeirut.org

Barbar 024
Rue Spears
T 01 379 779

Beirut Art Center 028
Building 13
Street 97
Jisr el-Wati
T 01 397 018
www.beirutartcenter.org

Bokja 078
Building 332
Mukhalissiye Street
T 01 975 576
www.bokjadesign.com

Burgundy 044
752 Gouraud Street
T 01 999 820
www.burgundybeirut.com

C

Camille Chamoun Stadium 088
Salim Salam
T 01 842 212
www.camillechamounsportscity.com

HOTELS
ADDRESSES AND ROOM RATES

Hotel Albergo 022
Room rates:
double, from $385;
Deluxe Suite, $560
Abdul Wahab el-Inglizi Street
T 01 339 797
www.albergobeirut.com

Le Bristol 016
Room rates:
double, from $275
Madame Curie Street
T 01 351 400
www.lebristol-hotel.com

Al Bustan 023
Room rates:
double, from $275
Beyt Meri
T 01 870 400
www.albustanhotel.com

Hotel Cavalier 016
Room rates:
double, from $120
Mohammad Abdul Baki Street
T 01 353 001
www.hotelcavalier.com

Four Seasons 017
Room rates:
double, from $305;
Diplomatic Suite, $2,780
1418 Wafik Sinno Avenue
T 01 761 000
www.fourseasons.com/beirut

Le Gray 018
Room rates:
double, from $390;
One-bedroom Corner Suite, $1,860
Weygand Street/Martyrs' Square
T 01 971 111
www.campbellgrayhotels.com

Hayete 016
Room rates:
double, from $100
Furn el-Hayek
www.hayete-guesthouse.com

The Mayflower 016
Room rates:
double, from $100
Nehme Yafet Street
T 01 340 680
www.mayflowerbeirut.com

Mir Amin 096
Room rates:
double, from $135
Shouf
T 70 103 222
www.miraminpalace.com

Phoenicia 020
Room rates:
double, from $330
Suleiman Frangieh Boulevard
T 01 369 100
www.phoeniciabeirut.com

35 Rooms 016
Room rates:
double, from $120
Baalbeck Street
T 01 345 676
www.35rooms.com

Le Vendôme 016
Room rates:
double, from $370
Ain el-Mreisse
T 01 369 280
www.ichotelsgroup.com

WALLPAPER* CITY GUIDES

Executive Editor
Rachael Moloney

Author
Warren Singh-Bartlett

Art Director
Loran Stosskopf
Art Editor
Eriko Shimazaki
Designer
Mayumi Hashimoto
Map Illustrator
Russell Bell

Photography Editor
Sophie Corben
Acting Photography Editor
Anika Burgess
Photography Assistant
Nabil Butt

Chief Sub-Editor
Nick Mee
Sub-Editor
Marie Cleland Knowles

Editorial Assistant
Emma Harrison

Interns
Carmen de Baets
Despina Rangou

**Wallpaper* Group
Editor-in-Chief**
Tony Chambers
Publishing Director
Gord Ray
Managing Editor
Jessica Diamond
Acting Managing Editor
Oliver Adamson

Contributor
Joseph Ghandour

Wallpaper* ® is a
registered trademark
of IPC Media Limited

First published 2012

All prices are correct at
the time of going to press,
but are subject to change.

Printed in China

PHAIDON

Phaidon Press Limited
Regent's Wharf
All Saints Street
London N1 9PA

Phaidon Press Inc
180 Varick Street
New York, NY 10014

Phaidon® is a registered
trademark of Phaidon
Press Limited

www.phaidon.com

A CIP Catalogue record for
this book is available from
the British Library.

© 2012 IPC Media Limited

ISBN 978 0 7148 6421 1

PHOTOGRAPHERS

Sindre Ellingsen/Alamy
Notre Dame du
Liban, pp070-071

Joe Kesrouani
Ixsir, p097

Nagib Khazaka
Beirut city view,
inside front cover
Abed Clocktower,
pp010-011
Statue of the Martyrs, p012
Hope of Peace
Monument, p013
St Georges
Hotel, pp014-015
Four Seasons, p017
Le Gray, p018, p019
Phoenicia, pp020-021
Hotel Albergo, p022
Al Bustan, p023
Gruen Eatery, p025
Beirut Souks, p026
National Museum, p027
Beirut Art
Center, pp028-029
STAY, p030
Music Hall, p031
Goutons Voir, p033
Sweet Tea, pp034-035

Chez Jean Claude, p036
Tawlet, p038
St Elmo's Seaside
Brasserie, p039
Ginette, pp040-041
L'Humeur du Chef, p042
Al Mayass, p043
Burgundy, pp044-045
Abdel Wahab, p046
Torino, p047
Cro Magnon, p048
Democratic Republic
of Music, p049
Chez Sami, pp050-051
Marinella, p052
Casablanca, p053
Lara Khoury, p055
Université Saint Joseph,
p057, pp058-059
Sursock Palace,
pp060-061
Interdesign Building, p062
The Egg, p063
Khashoggi Mosque,
pp064-065
Barakat Building,
pp066-067
Electricité du Liban
Building, p068
Gefinor Center, p069
Maison Rabih
Kayrouz, p073
Studio Karim
Bekdache, pp074-075

Orient 499, p076
Johnny Farah, p077
Bokja, pp078-079
Nada Debs, p080
XXieme Siècle, p082
Karen Chekerdjian, p083
STARCH, pp084-085
Papercup, p086
Senteurs d'Orient, p087
Corniche, p089
American University of
Beirut pool, pp091-092
Golf Club of Lebanon,
pp094-095

Warren Singh-Bartlett
Temple of Bacchus,
pp100-101

Simon Skreddernes
Rachid Karami
International
Fair, pp098-099

BEIRUT

A COLOUR-CODED GUIDE TO THE HOT 'HOODS

HAMRA/RAS BEIRUT
Its chic modernist heyday is over, but Hamra still buzzes with a diverse mix of Beirutis

GEMMAYZE/MAR MIKHAYEL
New life is coursing through these downtown areas, centred on lively Gouraud Street

MOUSSEITBEH/MAZRAA
These dense suburbs are fringed by the city's pinewood park and one useable beach

QANTARI
Ravaged during the wars, this old district is now sought-after and developing upwards

CENTRAL BEIRUT
Extensive regeneration is slowly returning the city's heart to its glorious former state

ZOUQAQ EL-BLATT/BASTA
The grand houses in this once wealthy and culturally rich district have fallen into decay

AIN EL-MREISSE
More than just the AUB campus, Beirut's coastal strip boasts the Corniche and super views

ASHRAFIYE
Undergoing rapid urbanisation, this district now offers eateries, boutiques and bars

For a full description of each neighbourhood, see the Introduction.
Featured venues are colour-coded, according to the district in which they are located.